number cakes

THE AUSTRALIAN Women's Weekly

contents

Bring a smile to your child's face with one of these fantastic number birthday cakes – they'll love you for it. And don't stress about needing to buy every cake pan. The number-shaped cake pans we used for most of these recipes are available for hire from cake decorating stores – check online for local stockists.

Pamela Clark

Editorial & Food Director

Australian cup and spoon measurements are metric. A conversion chart appears on page 78.

one lullaby bear

equipment

- two 8cm x 25cm (3¼-inch x 10-inch) bar cake pans
- 23cm x 51cm (9¼-inch x 20½-inch) rectangular cake board (page 68)
- rolling pin
- pastry wheel
- ruler
- tiny moon-, star- and heart-shaped cutters

cake

- 1 x 340g (11-ounce) packet butter cake mix
- 1 quantity butter cream (page 65)
- blue food colouring

decorations

- icing (confectioners') sugar, for dusting
- 250g (8 ounces) ready-made white icing
- yellow, green and pink food colouring
- 22 coloured cachous
- small teddy bear or doll

1 Preheat oven to 180°C/350°F. Grease and line cake pans.

2 Make cake according to directions on packet; divide mixture evenly between pans. Bake about 25 minutes. Stand cakes in pans 5 minutes; turn onto a wire rack to cool. Using a serrated knife, level cake tops to the same height.

3 Cut one cake into three pieces (see page 72). Assemble cake pieces on board, cut-side down, to form number 1; discard remaining cake. Secure cake pieces to board with a little butter cream.

4 Tint butter cream blue; spread all over cake.

5 On surface dusted with a little icing sugar, knead ready-made icing until smooth. Roll half the icing until 3mm (⅛-inch) thick, cut a 11cm (4½-inch) square for the sheet; cover sheet and enclose white trimmings in plastic wrap.

6 Knead yellow colouring into remaining icing; roll until 3mm (⅛-inch) thick. Using pastry wheel and ruler, cut a 10cm (4-inch) square for the quilt; enclose yellow trimmings in plastic wrap. Using ruler, mark 2.5cm (1-inch) intervals on all four quilt edges. Using pastry wheel, ruler and markings as guides, gently roll wheel across icing to make quilt pattern.

7 Using tiny cutters or a sharp-pointed knife, cut moon and star shapes from quilt; cover quilt with plastic wrap. Position shapes at top of cake with 10 of the cachous; shape yellow trimmings into a pillow, place on cake. Position sheet on cake, top with quilt; turn down the edge.

8 Divide reserved white trimmings in half. Knead green colouring into one half and pink into the other half; roll each until 3mm (⅛-inch) thick. Using tiny cutters or a sharp-pointed knife, cut heart shapes; position on cake with remaining cachous. Position teddy bear or doll near pillow.

tips One-year-olds may be too young to eat the cachous, but they'll certainly love the cake. Tiny moon-, star-, heart- and other-shaped cutters are sometimes sold as aspic cutters.

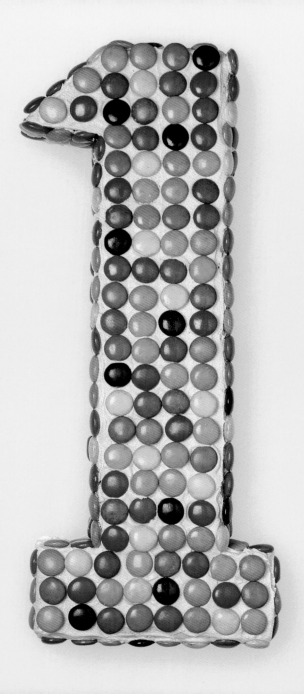

tip One-year-olds may be too young to eat these colourful Smarties, but they will love the cake.

smartie one

equipment

- two 8cm x 25cm (3¼-inch x 10-inch) bar cake pan
- 23cm x 51cm (9¼-inch x 20½-inch) rectangular cake board (page 68)

cake

- 1 x 340g (11-ounce) packet butter cake mix
- 1 quantity butter cream (page 65)
- yellow food colouring

decorations

- 4 x 100g (3-ounce) packets Smarties

1 Preheat oven to 180°C/350°F. Grease and line cake pans.

2 Make cake according to directions on packet; divide mixture evenly between pans. Bake about 25 minutes. Stand cakes in pans 5 minutes; turn onto a wire rack to cool. Using a serrated knife, level cake tops to the same height.

3 Cut one cake into three pieces (see page 72). Assemble cake pieces on board, cut-side down, to form number 1; discard remaining cake. Secure cake pieces to board with a little butter cream.

4 Tint butter cream yellow; spread all over cake. Using the picture as a guide, cover top and sides with Smarties.

one mother duck cupcakes

equipment

- **12-hole (⅓-cup/80ml) standard muffin pan**
- **6 blue muffin paper cases**
- **3.5cm (1½-inch) and 6.5cm (2¾-inch) wide duck-shaped cutters**
- **small new artist's paint brush**
- **20cm x 50cm (8-inch x 20-inch) rectangular cake board (page 68)**

cake

- **½ x 340g (11-ounce) packet butter cake mix**
- **½ quantity butter cream (page 65)**
- **yellow, orange and blue food colouring**

decorations

- **100g (3-ounce) ready-made white icing**
- **pure icing (confectioners') sugar, for dusting**
- **6 blue rainbow choc-chips**

1 Preheat oven to 180°C/350°F. Line six holes of the muffin pan with paper cases.

2 Make cake according to directions on packet. Drop 2½ level tablespoons of mixture into each case; bake about 20 minutes. Stand cakes in pan 5 minutes before turning, top-side up, onto a wire rack to cool.

3 Knead ready-made icing on surface dusted with a little sifted icing sugar until icing loses its stickiness; tint yellow. Roll icing on surface dusted with sifted icing sugar into a 3mm (⅛-inch) thickness. Using cutters, cut two large ducks and five small ducks from the icing. Brush one side of a large duck sparingly, but evenly, with water. Gently press the other large duck onto the damp surface.

4 Using the paint brush and orange food colouring, paint an orange beak on each side of the mother duck's head. Gently press a blue rainbow choc-chip into the icing to make an eye. Lay mother duck flat on a baking-paper-lined tray to dry. Paint beaks and position eyes on ducklings; dry on tray with mother duck.

5 Tint butter cream blue; spread over tops of cakes. Position cakes on cake board to form the number 1; secure with a little butter cream. Position mother duck and ducklings on cakes.

tips Make a duckling-topped cake for each small guest – even though they might not be eating the cakes they'll love the look of them. Make sure the ducks are completely dry and firm. The drying time will depend on the weather; if it's wet or humid, it could take overnight. The ducklings will take less time to dry than the mother duck. Use the whole cake mix to make extra cakes for the party.

tips Be sure to remove the toothpicks from the cake before cutting and serving. If you are unable to get the green licorice allsort you can use a blue one or any similar shaped lolly you like.

taller at two

equipment
- **15cm x 34cm (6-inch x 13½-inch) number 2 cake pan**
- **35cm x 45cm (14-inch x 18-inch) rectangular cake board (page 68)**

cake
- **2 x 340g (11-ounce) packets butter cake mix**
- **2 quantities butter cream (page 65)**
- **orange and yellow food colouring**
- **¼ cup (25g) cocoa powder**

decorations
- **¼ cup (55g) white (granulated) sugar**
- **1 black licorice strap**
- **1 white marshmallow**
- **1 green licorice allsort**
- **blue glossy decorating gel**
- **2 double-pointed toothpicks**
- **2 spearmint leaves**
- **2 chocolate finger biscuits**

1 Preheat oven to 180°C/350°F. Grease cake pan; line base with baking paper.

2 Make cakes according to directions on packets; pour mixture into pan. Bake about 45 minutes. Stand in pan 5 minutes before turning, top-side up, onto a wire rack to cool.

3 Using a serrated knife, level cake top; place cake, cut-side down, on cake board, securing with a little butter cream.

4 Tint three-quarters of the butter cream orange; spread all over cake.

5 Place sugar and yellow colouring in a small plastic bag; rub until sugar is evenly coloured. Sprinkle over cake.

6 Combine remaining butter cream and sifted cocoa in a small bowl. Dollop teaspoons of butter cream onto cake, flatten with the back of spoon to resemble giraffe markings.

7 Cut licorice strap into thin strips; position strips to outline cake and mouth.

8 Cut marshmallow in half, discard one half; place green allsort on top of remaining half. Pipe a dot with decorating gel on allsort to complete eye; position on head.

9 Insert toothpicks into the base of spearmint leaves; press into head for ears. Position biscuits next to spearmint leaves to resemble horns.

butterfly two

- deep 26cm x 36cm (10½-inch x 14½-inch) baking dish
- 12-hole (2-tablespoon/40ml) deep flat-based patty pan
- 12 patty pan paper cases
- 35cm x 45cm (14-inch x 18-inch) rectangular cake board (page 68)

cake

- 3 x 340g (11-ounce) packets butter cake mix
- 2 quantities butter cream (page 65)
- red and blue food colouring

decorations

- 12 yellow jelly beans
- 24 chocolate freckles
- 1 yellow fruit stick
- 15 marshmallows
- 6 Smarties

1 Preheat oven to 180°C/350°F. Grease and line baking dish; line patty pan with paper cases.

2 Make cakes according to directions on packets. Drop 2 tablespoons of mixture into each paper case; pour remaining mixture into baking dish. Bake patty cakes about 20 minutes and large cake about 1 hour. Stand cakes 5 minutes before turning, top-side up, onto wire racks to cool.

3 Using a serrated knife, level top of large cake. Secure cake, cut-side down, to board with a little butter cream.

4 Tint two-thirds of the butter cream red; spread all over large cake. Tint remaining butter cream blue; spread over tops of patty cakes.

5 Position 2 jelly beans on 6 patty cakes for butterfly bodies; position freckles for butterfly wings. Cut fruit stick into small thin strips; position for butterfly antennae.

6 Using a pair of scissors, cut marshmallows in half; pinch marshmallow ends together to form petals. Position Smarties on remaining patty cakes for flower buds; position marshmallows for petals.

7 Position patty cakes on large cake to form the number 2.

jigsaw two

equipment

- **15cm x 34cm (6-inch x 13½-inch) number 2 cake pan**
- **25cm x 43cm (10-inch x 17-inch) rectangular cake board (page 68)**

cake

- **2 x 340g (11-ounce) packets butter cake mix**
- **1 quantity butter cream (page 65)**

decorations

- **2 x 125g (4-ounce) packets coloured cake sprinkles**

1 Preheat oven to 180°C/350°F. Grease cake pan; line base with baking paper.

2 Make cakes according to directions on packets; pour mixture into pan. Bake about 45 minutes. Stand in pan 5 minutes before turning, top-side up, onto a wire rack to cool.

3 Using a serrated knife, level top of cake. Cut jigsaw-shaped pieces from cake (see page 72).

4 Keeping colours separate, empty cake sprinkles on to five pieces of baking paper. Work with one jigsaw piece at a time: spread top and the side(s) that will show with butter cream; roll in one of the sprinkle colours then position on cake board; spread a little more butter cream on the uniced side(s) that will join with the next jigsaw piece. Continue until all pieces are coloured and fitted together.

pretty polka dot three

- **23cm x 34cm (9-inch x 13½-inch) number 3 cake pan**
- **30cm x 40cm (12-inch x 16-inch) rectangular cake board (page 68)**
- **7cm (2¾-inch) round cutter**

cake

- **2 x 340g (11-ounce) packets butter cake mix**
- **1 quantity fluffy frosting (page 65)**
- **pink food colouring**

decorations

- **16 white chocolate Melts**

1 Preheat oven to 180°C/350°F. Grease cake pan; line base with baking paper.

2 Make cakes according to directions on packets; spread mixture into pan. Bake about 45 minutes. Stand in pan 5 minutes before turning, top-side up, onto a wire rack to cool.

3 Using a serrated knife, level cake top; place cake, cut-side down, on cake board, securing with a little frosting.

4 Tint fluffy frosting pink; spread all over cake.

5 Using the cutter, cut through about half the chocolate Melts to make the edges rounded. Using the picture as a guide, decorate cake with Melts.

tips To keep the glossy finish to the frosting, the cake needs to be frosted no longer than 1 hour before the party. The frosting soon dries out, resembling cooked meringue. When assembling the number 3 cake pan make sure the metal insert is put in on the opposite side, so when the cake is turned upside down it makes a 3. Otherwise you'll have to decorate the cut side of the cake.

tip If you are unable to buy apricot Roll-Ups use your favourite flavour.

fishes for three

equipment

- 23cm x 34cm (9-inch x 13½-inch) number 3 cake pan
- 25cm x 40cm (10-inch x 16-inch) rectangular cake board (page 68)

cake

- 2 x 340g (11-ounce) packets butter cake mix
- 2 quantities butter cream (page 65)
- blue food colouring

decorations

- 2 teaspoons white (granulated) sugar
- 4 apricot fruit Roll-Ups
- 36 blue Smarties
- 1 black licorice strap
- 4 Mentos
- red glossy decorating gel
- 5 ice-cream wafers
- 1 tablespoon orange sprinkles

1 Preheat oven to 180°C/350°F. Grease cake pan; line base with baking paper.

2 Make cakes according to directions on packets; pour mixture into pan. Bake about 45 minutes. Stand in pan 5 minutes before turning top-side up onto a wire rack to cool.

3 Using a serrated knife, level cake top; place cake, cut-side down, on cake board, securing with a little butter cream.

4 Tint one-third of the butter cream pale blue; tint remaining butter cream a darker blue. Using the picture as a guide, spread pale blue butter cream over both ends of the cake. Reserve 1 tablespoon of the darker blue butter cream; spread remainder over the rest of the cake.

5 Place sugar and blue colouring in a small plastic bag; rub until sugar is evenly coloured. Sprinkle over pale blue butter cream.

6 Cut two Roll-Ups into four fin-shaped pieces. Form two fins by joining pieces together with a little water, trim if needed. Place fins at the start of the dark blue section on each end. Cut two 5cm x 9cm (2-inch x 3¾-inch) triangles from Roll-Ups; join together with a little water, place on cake at centre of the figure for a tail. Cut four 1cm x 6cm (½-inch x 2½-inch) strips from remaining Roll-Ups, shape one end into a curve; join two pieces with a little water. Place on cake as mouths.

7 Position Smarties on dark blue butter cream for scales. Cut licorice strap into thin strips; position on cake to outline fins, tails and mouths. Place Mentos on heads for eyes, pipe with red decorating gel.

8 Cut wafers in half on the diagonal; position two pieces for heads and eight pieces for spines. Spread reserved butter cream on wafers; cover with orange sprinkles.

creepy crawly three

equipment

- 23cm x 34cm (9¼-inch x 13½-inch) number 3 cake pan
- 12-hole (2-tablespoon/40ml) flat-based patty pan
- 9 patty pan paper cases
- 25cm x 40cm (10-inch x 16-inch) rectangular cake board (page 68)

cake

- 3 x 340g (11-ounce) packets butter cake mix
- 2 quantities butter cream (page 65)
- blue and yellow food colouring

decorations

- ½ cup (35g) shredded coconut
- 16 dark pink jelly beans
- 1 white Mallow Bake
- black glossy decorating gel
- 5cm (2-inch) piece black licorice strap

1 Preheat oven to 180°C/350°F. Grease cake pan; line base with baking paper. Line 9 patty pan holes with paper cases.

2 Make cakes according to directions on packets. Place 2 tablespoons of mixture in each paper case; pour remaining mixture into cake pan. Bake patty cakes about 20 minutes and number cake about 45 minutes. Stand in pans 5 minutes before turning top-side up, onto wire racks to cool.

3 Using a serrated knife, level top of number cake. Secure cake, cut-side down, to board with a little butter cream.

4 Tint three-quarters of the butter cream blue; spread all over number cake. Tint remaining butter cream yellow; spread on tops of patty cakes.

5 Place coconut and yellow colouring in a plastic bag; rub until coconut is evenly coloured. Dip tops of eight patty cakes in coconut; position on number cake to form caterpillar body. Position jelly beans for feet.

6 Using a pair of scissors, cut Mallow Bake in half; position on remaining patty cake for eyes. Using decorating gel, pipe dots on mallow bakes for pupils.

7 Cut licorice strap lengthways into three strips; tie a knot in the end of two of the strips and position on patty cake for antennae. Trim remaining strip and position to form mouth; discard remaining licorice strip.

tip Cut colourful fruit sticks to any length for a variety of uses. They can be legs or arms, or form a colourful outline of a shape on your cake. They are available from supermarkets.

stripy four

equipment

- 23cm x 34cm (9¼-inch x 13½-inch) number 4 cake pan
- 25cm x 40cm (10-inch x 16-inch) rectangular cake board (page 68)

cake

- 3 x 340g (11-ounce) packets butter cake mix
- 1 quantity butter cream (page 65)
- blue food colouring

decorations

- 7 pink fruit sticks
- 6 orange fruit sticks
- 6 green fruit sticks
- 6 yellow fruit sticks

1 Preheat oven to 180°C/350°F. Grease cake pan; line base with baking paper.

2 Make cakes according to directions on packets; pour mixture into pan. Bake about 50 minutes. Stand in pan 5 minutes before turning, top-side up, onto a wire rack to cool.

3 Using a serrated knife, level cake top; place cake cut-side down, on cake board, securing with a little butter cream.

4 Tint butter cream blue; spread all over cake.

5 Using a sharp pair of scissors, trim each fruit stick to fit across cake. Using the picture as a guide, decorate cake with fruit sticks.

spotty four

equipment

- **23cm x 34cm (9¼-inch x 13½-inch) number 4 cake pan**
- **25cm x 40cm (10-inch x 16-inch) rectangular cake board (page 68)**

cake

- **3 x 340g (11-ounce) packets butter cake mix**
- **2 quantities butter cream (page 65)**
- **green food colouring**

decorations

- **16 Kool Fruits**
- **21 Smarties**

1 Preheat oven to 180°C/350°F. Grease cake pan, line base with baking paper.

2 Make cakes according to directions on packets; pour mixture into pan. Bake about 50 minutes. Stand in pan 5 minutes before turning top-side up, onto a wire rack to cool.

3 Using a serrated knife, level cake top; place cake cut-side down, on cake board, securing with a little butter cream.

4 Tint butter cream green; spread all over cake.

5 Using the picture as a guide, decorate cake with Kool Fruits and Smarties.

tips You can decorate this cake with single- or multi-coloured lollies. Place lollies such as Smarties on butter cream close to presentation time to prevent the colours running.

artistic four

equipment

- 23cm x 34cm (9¼-inch x 13½-inch) number 4 cake pan
- 25cm x 40cm (10-inch x 16-inch) rectangular cake board (page 68)

cake

- 3 x 340g (11-ounce) packets butter cake mix
- 1 quantity fluffy frosting (page 65)
- orange, yellow, blue, green and pink food colouring

decorations

- small paint brush

1 Preheat oven to 180°C/350°F. Grease cake pan; line base with baking paper.

2 Make cakes according to directions on packets; pour mixture into pan. Bake about 50 minutes. Stand in pan 5 minutes before turning top-side up, onto a wire rack to cool.

3 Using a serrated knife, level top of the cake. Place cake cut-side down on cake board; secure with a little frosting.

4 Reserve 1 cup frosting; spread remaining frosting all over cake.

5 Divide reserved frosting into five small bowls; tint each bowl with one of the suggested colours – orange, yellow, blue, green and pink.

6 Using the picture as a guide, dollop spoonfuls of coloured frosting onto the cake; position paint brush on cake.

superstar five

- 3cm (1¼-inch) five-pointed star cutter
- 5cm (2-inch) six-pointed star cutter
- eight 10cm (4-inch) lengths florists' wire
- oven tray
- 20cm x 34cm (8-inch x 13½-inch) number 5 cake pan
- 25cm x 40cm (10-inch x 16-inch) rectangular cake board (page 68)

cake

- 2 x 340g (11-ounce) packets butter cake mix
- 1½ quantities butter cream (page 65)
- yellow food colouring

decorations

- 200g (6½ ounces) ready-made white icing
- 2 tablespoons pure icing (confectioners') sugar
- blue food colouring

1 Knead ready-made icing on surface dusted with sifted icing sugar until icing loses its stickiness; divide icing in half. Tint one portion blue; tint other portion a darker blue. Roll out each colour, one at a time, until 5mm (¼-inch) thick. Using both star cutters, cut out star shapes from both icings.

2 Using the picture as a guide, bend and curl lengths of florists' wire. Wet one end of each length of wire; push damp ends into sides of some of the smaller stars. Place stars on a baking-paper-lined tray; stand overnight to dry.

3 Preheat oven to 180°C/350°F. Grease cake pan; line base with baking paper.

4 Make cakes according to directions on packets; pour mixture into pan. Bake about 45 minutes. Stand in pan 5 minutes before turning top-side up, onto a wire rack to cool.

5 Using a serrated knife, level cake top; place cake cut-side down, on cake board, securing with a little butter cream.

6 Tint butter cream yellow; spread all over cake.

7 Using the picture as a guide, position stars on cake.

tips While the stars need to be made a day ahead to dry, the cake can also be made and covered with butter cream the day before to make it easier on party day. Decorate the cake with stars up to 3 hours before the party.

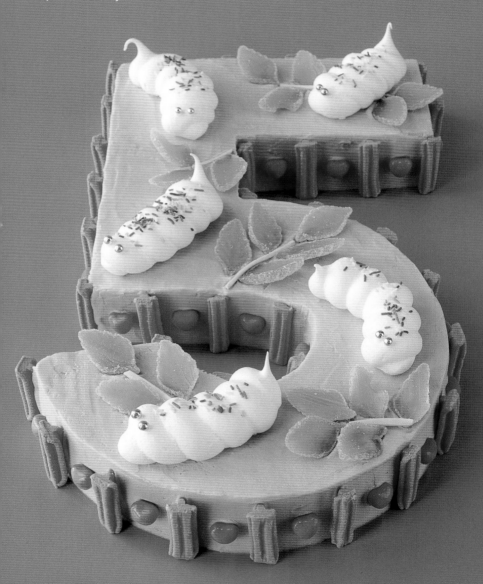

tips Grubs can be made up to a week ahead; store them in an airtight container. You can use any heart shaped sweets, if you can't find the love hearts.

five meringue grubs

equipment

- oven tray
- 20cm x 34cm (8-inch x 13½-inch) number 5 cake pan
- 25cm x 40cm (10-inch x 16-inch) rectangular cake board (page 68)

meringue grubs

- 1 egg white
- ¾ cup (165g) caster (superfine) sugar
- ¼ teaspoon cream of tartar
- 2 tablespoons boiling water
- large piping bag fitted with 1cm (½-inch) plain tube
- coloured cake sprinkles
- 10 coloured cachous

cake

- 1 x 340g (11-ounce) packet butter cake mix
- 1½ quantities butter cream (page 65)
- pink food colouring

decorations

- 36 mini pink musk sticks
- 36 love hearts
- 1 green fruit stick
- 11 mint leaves

1 Preheat oven to 120°C/250°F. Line oven tray with baking paper.

2 To make meringue grubs: combine egg white, sugar, cream of tartar and the boiling water in a small heatproof bowl. Place bowl over a small saucepan of simmering water (make sure the base of the bowl does not touch the water). Beat egg-white mixture with an electric mixer 7 minutes or until sugar is dissolved and stiff peaks form. Remove bowl from heat; spoon egg-white mixture immediately into the piping bag. Pipe five grubs onto oven tray. Top grubs with coloured sprinkles; position cachous on grubs for eyes. Bake 30 minutes or until grubs are dry to touch; cool.

3 Increase oven to 180°C/350°F. Grease cake pan; line base with baking paper.

4 Make cake according to directions on packet; pour mixture into pan. Bake about 45 minutes. Stand in pan 5 minutes before turning top-side up, onto a wire rack to cool.

5 Using a serrated knife, level cake top; place cut-side down on cake board, securing with a little butter cream.

6 Tint butter cream pink; spread all over cake.

7 Position meringue grubs on cake; decorate sides of cake with musk sticks and love hearts. Thinly slice fruit stick lengthways; position on cake for stems. Using a sharp knife, cut mint leaves in half horizontally; cut a few 'nibbles' out of a leaf or two. Position leaves on cake.

purr-fect five

equipment

- 12-hole (⅓-cup/80ml) standard muffin pan
- 11 orange standard muffin paper cases
- 35cm x 45cm (14-inch x 18-inch) rectangular cake board (page 68)

cake

- 1 x 340g (11-ounce) packet butter cake mix
- ½ quantity butter cream (page 65)
- orange and pink food colouring

decorations

- 4 x 35g (1-ounce) tubes mini M&M's
- 3 small pink jelly beans, halved crossways
- 1 musk stick
- 1 red sour strap
- 10 large pink candy hearts

1 Preheat oven to 180°C/350°C. Line muffin pan with the paper cases.

2 Make cake according to directions on packet; drop 2½ level tablespoons of the mixture into each paper case. Bake about 20 minutes. Stand in pan 5 minutes before turning, top-side up, onto a wire rack to cool.

3 Divide butter cream into two small bowls; tint one bowl orange and the other bowl pink. Spread orange butter cream over the tops of five cakes; spread pink butter cream over remaining six cakes.

4 Using the picture as a guide, position cakes on cake board to resemble the number 5; secure with a little butter cream. Decorate each pink cake using orange mini M&M's to make heart shapes.

5 Decorate the five remaining kitty face cakes using pink mini M&M's for eyes and jelly bean halves for noses. Cut musk stick into thin strips; cut strips into 20 x 2.5cm (1-inch) lengths to use as whiskers. Cut sour strap into 10 x 2cm (¾-inch) strips; shape and position two strips for each mouth. Position candy hearts for ears on each kitty.

tip You'll have about 1 cup of the cake mixture left over; use it to make extra cakes for the party.

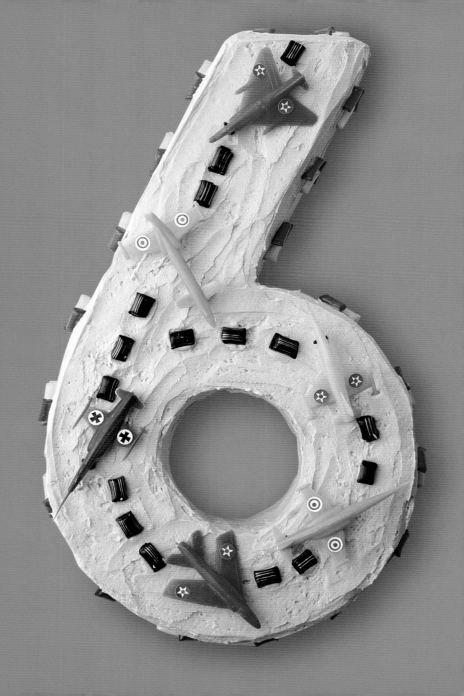

six jet planes

equipment
- 22cm x 34cm (9-inch x 13½-inch) number 6 cake pan
- 25cm x 40cm (10-inch x 16-inch) rectangular cake board (page 68)

cake
- 3 x 340g (11-ounce) packets butter cake mix
- 1 quantity butter cream (page 65)
- green food colouring

decorations
- red, yellow and black sweets
- 6 plastic aeroplanes

1 Preheat oven to 180°C/350°F. Grease cake pan; line base with baking paper.

2 Make cakes according to directions on packets; pour mixture into pan. Bake about 50 minutes. Stand in pan 5 minutes before turning top-side up, onto a wire rack to cool.

3 Using a serrated knife, level cake top; place cake cut-side down on cake board, securing with a little frosting.

4 Tint butter cream green. Spread all over cake. Decorate sides with red and yellow sweets to form arrows, decorate top with black sweets to create a runway. Using the picture as a guide, position planes on cake.

tip If you can't purchase the red, yellow and black sweets you could use jelly beans or Smarties.

slithering six

equipment

- 22cm x 34cm (9-inch x 13½-inch) number 6 cake pan
- 25cm x 40cm (10-inch x 16-inch) rectangular cake board (page 68)

cake

- 3 x 340g (11-ounce) packets butter cake mix
- 2 quantities butter cream (page 65)
- purple food colouring

decorations

- 125g (4 ounces) ready-made white icing
- 2 tablespoons pure icing (confectioners') sugar
- yellow food colouring
- 1 white marshmallow
- 22 yellow Smarties
- 36 purple Smarties
- 5cm (2-inch) piece black licorice strap

1 Preheat oven to 180°C/350°F. Grease cake pan; line base with baking paper.

2 Make cakes according to directions on packets; pour mixture into pan. Bake about 50 minutes. Stand in pan 5 minutes before turning top-side up, onto a wire rack to cool.

3 Using a serrated knife, level cake top. Cut through the number six where it meets at the centre, trim and shape the cake to make the snake's head. Place cake cut side down on cake board; secure with a little frosting.

4 Tint three-quarters of the butter cream purple; spread all over cake, leaving the snake's head uniced. Tint remaining butter cream dark purple; spread over snake's head.

5 Knead ready-made icing on surface dusted with sifted icing sugar until icing loses its stickiness; tint yellow. Divide icing into five portions; roll each portion into a 5mm (¼-inch) rope. Using picture as a guide, position ropes across snake's body; trim ends.

6 Cut marshmallow in half horizontally. Using picture as a guide, position marshmallows, cut-side up, for eyes; top each with a yellow Smartie. Position remaining Smarties across snake's body to represent bands. Cut a small triangle from one end of the licorice strap, position on cake for snake's tongue.

tip The cake can be completed a day before the party.

tip If you can't buy green Bubble Tape, you can use grape Bubble Tape or Roll-Ups.

six little devils

- 22cm x 34cm (9-inch x 13½-inch) number 6 cake pan
- 25cm x 40cm (10-inch x 16-inch) rectangular cake board (page 68)

- 3 x 340g (11-ounce) packets butter cake mix
- 2 quantities butter cream (page 65)
- black and red food colouring

- 2 banana lollies
- 8cm (3¼-inch) green Bubble Tape (bubble gum)
- 1 black licorice strap
- 2 green M&M's
- 1 milk bottle, halved lengthways

1 Preheat oven to 180°C/350°F. Grease cake pan; line base with baking paper.

2 Make cakes according to directions on packets; pour mixture into pan. Bake about 50 minutes. Stand in pan 5 minutes before turning top-side up, onto a wire rack to cool.

3 Using a serrated knife, level cake top. Using the picture as a guide, shape the top of the six into a tail (see page 72). Place cake, cut-side down, on cake board, securing with a little butter cream.

4 Tint a quarter of the butter cream with black colouring; spread on cake over widow's peak and end of tail. Tint remaining butter cream red; spread over remaining cake.

5 Trim banana ends diagonally; position on cake for horns. Cut eyes from Bubble Tape; position on cake. Cut 8cm (3¼-inch) piece from licorice strap; outline eyes. Position M&M's on cake for eye irises.

6 Cut eyebrows, mouth and goatee from remaining licorice strap; position on cake. Trim milk bottle halves for fangs; position on cake.

adventurous seven

equipment

- 12-hole (⅓-cup/80ml) standard muffin pan
- 5 blue standard muffin paper cases
- 4 green standard muffin paper cases
- 30cm x 45cm (12-inch x 18-inch) rectangular cake board (page 68)

cake

- 1 x 340g (11-ounce) packet butter cake mix
- ½ quantity butter cream (page 65)
- blue and green food colouring

decorations

- 2 tablespoons desiccated coconut
- 7 After-dinner Mints
- 13 scorched peanuts
- 1 teaspoon red, orange and yellow BoPeep lollies, chopped coarsely
- 1 red jelly baby
- 1 mint leaf, sliced finely
- 3 small plastic crocodile toys
- 1 plastic tree
- 1 x 30cm (12-inch) green chenille stick (pipe cleaner)
- 1 x 30cm (12-inch) piece red licorice bootlace
- 1 yellow fruit stick

1 Preheat oven to 180°C/350°F. Line muffin pan with the paper cases.

2 Make cake according to directions on packet; drop 2½ level tablespoons of mixture into each paper case. Bake about 20 minutes. Stand in pan 5 minutes before turning top-side up, onto a wire rack to cool.

3 Divide butter cream into two small bowls; tint one blue and the other green. Spread blue butter cream on cakes in blue cases; spread green butter cream on cakes in green cases. Position on cake board to form the number 7; secure each with a little butter cream.

4 Place coconut and a few drops of green colouring in a small plastic bag; rub until coconut is evenly coloured. Using picture as a guide, sprinkle coconut over cakes to make grass.

5 Working quickly, use a hot metal spatula to melt one edge on two After-dinner Mints; pressing gently, join the melted edges together on an angle for part of the tent. Repeat with two more After-dinner Mints; position tent on cakes.

6 Using picture as a guide, use some of the scorched peanuts and chopped BoPeeps to make a campfire; position jelly baby near the fire. Position slices of mint leaf for water reeds; position crocodiles and the tree. Use remaining scorched peanuts for rocks. Shape two After-dinner Mints into rock platforms; place at the water's edge.

7 For the flying fox, cut small pieces of the chenille stick and use to secure one end of the licorice bootlace to the plastic tree and the other end of the bootlace to a small segment of the fruit stick. Gently push the fruit stick into one of the green cakes. Shape a small piece of the chenille stick to make flying fox handle bars; position on the licorice bootlace. Trim the remaining After-dinner Mint into a platform at the end of the flying fox.

tips Use left over cake mixture to make extra cakes for the party. If you are unable to buy BoPeep lollies, crush any red and yellow boiled lollies. Kids love to go camping. If you have a large enough grassed area at home, turn the area into a camping ground for the party. It's an easy, inexpensive party theme.

floral seven

equipment
- 20cm x 34cm (8-inch x 13½-inch) number 7 cake pan
- 25cm x 40cm (10-inch x 16-inch) rectangular cake board (page 68)

cake
- 2 x 340g (11-ounce) packets butter cake mix
- 1 quantity fluffy frosting (page 65)

decorations
- 14 ready-made yellow and white sugar flowers

1 Preheat oven to 180°C/350°F. Grease cake pan; line base with baking paper.

2 Make cakes according to directions on packets; pour mixture into pan. Bake about 45 minutes. Stand in pan 5 minutes before turning top-side up, onto a wire rack to cool.

3 Using a serrated knife, level cake top; place cake, cut-side down on cake board, securing with a little frosting.

4 Spread the remaining frosting all over cake. Using picture as a guide, position flowers on cake.

tip To keep the glossy finish to the frosting, the cake needs to be frosted no longer than 1 hour before the party. The frosting soon dries out, resembling cooked meringue.

seven choc-crackle spiders

equipment

- two 12-hole (1-tablespoon/20ml) mini muffin pans
- 20cm x 34cm (8-inch x 13½-inch) number 7 cake pan
- 25cm x 40cm (10-inch x 16-inch) rectangular cake board (page 68)
- piping bag fitted with 2mm (⅛-inch) plain tube

choc-crackle spiders

- 1 cup (35g) Rice Bubbles
- 1 cup (70g) shredded coconut
- 1 tablespoon cocoa powder
- 1 tablespoon icing (confectioners') sugar
- 100g (3 ounces) dark (semi-sweet) chocolate, melted
- 30g (1-ounce) butter, melted

cake

- 2 x 340g (11-ounce) packets butter cake mix
- 1½ quantities butter cream (page 65)
- orange and black food colouring

decorations

- 28 x 15cm (6-inch) black chenille sticks (pipe cleaners)
- 14 Skittles

1 For the choc-crackle spiders, combine Rice Bubbles, coconut, sifted cocoa and icing sugar in a medium bowl. Using a fork, stir in chocolate and butter. Spoon level tablespoons of mixture into muffin pan holes. Refrigerate about 1 hour or until spiders have set.

2 Preheat oven to 180°C/350°F. Grease cake pan; line base with baking paper.

3 Make cakes according to directions on packets; pour mixture into pan. Bake about 45 minutes. Stand in pan 5 minutes before turning top-side up, onto a wire rack to cool.

4 Using a serrated knife, level cake top; place cake, cut-side down, on cake board, securing with a little butter cream.

5 Tint three-quarters of the butter cream orange; spread all over cake. Tint remaining butter cream black; spoon into piping bag. Pipe spider webs onto cake and board.

6 Twist four chenille sticks together at the centre; bend the ends to make spider legs. Position legs on cake; top with one spider body.

7 Using leftover butter cream, attach Skittles onto spider for eyes; pipe a little black icing on Skittles for pupils. Repeat with remaining chenille sticks, spider bodies, black butter cream and skittles.

tips Chocolate and butter can be melted together over hot water or in a microwave on HIGH (100%) for about 1 minute. This recipe makes 24 choc-crackle spiders, however, the decorations are for the 7 spiders on the cake. If you have extra chenille sticks and Skittles, decorate the extra choc-crackles to give to each guest.

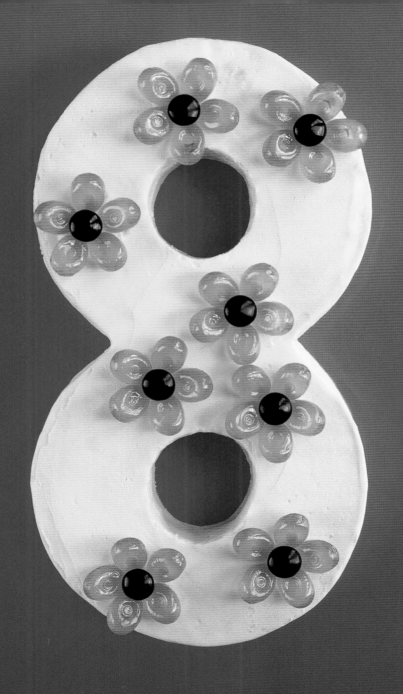

tip You can use any coloured oval boiled lollies you like — why not use the birthday girl's favourite colour?

eight little flowers

equipment

- 23cm x 34cm (9¼-inch x 13½-inch) number 8 cake pan
- 25cm x 40cm (10-inch x 16-inch) rectangular cake board (page 68)

cake

- 3 x 340g (11-ounce) packets butter cake mix
- 2 quantities butter cream (page 65)
- yellow food colouring

decorations

- 40 boiled lollies
- 8 giant black Smarties

1 Preheat oven to 180°C/350°F. Grease cake pan; line base with baking paper.

2 Make cakes according to directions on packets; pour mixture into pan. Bake about 1 hour. Stand in pan 5 minutes before turning top-side up, onto a wire rack to cool.

3 Using a serrated knife, level cake top; place cake, cut-side down, on cake board, securing with a little butter cream.

4 Tint butter cream yellow; spread all over cake.

5 Using picture as a guide, arrange boiled lollies and Smarties on the cake into flowers.

eight on the road

equipment

- 2 x 12-hole (⅓-cup/80ml) standard muffin pans
- 16 yellow standard muffin paper cases
- 30cm x 45cm (12-inch x 18-inch) rectangular cake board (page 68)

cake

- 1 x 340g (11-ounce) packet butter cake mix
- 1 quantity butter cream (page 65)
- blue food colouring
- ⅓ cup (35g) cocoa powder

decorations

- 1 x 55g (2-ounce) Cherry Ripe bar
- 2 x 25g (¾-ounce) Curly Wurly bars
- 1 roll black licorice strap
- 1 jelly baby
- 2 red mini M&M's
- 2 yellow mini M&M's
- 2 green mini M&M's
- 2 ice-block sticks
- 1 large round green jube
- small toy vehicles

1 Preheat oven to 180°C/350°F. Line muffin pan with the paper cases.
2 Make cake according to directions on packet; drop 2½ level tablespoons of mixture into each paper case. Bake about 20 minutes. Stand cakes in pan 5 minutes before turning, top-side up, onto a wire rack to cool.
3 Place 2 tablespoons of butter cream into a small bowl; tint blue. Stir sifted cocoa into remaining butter cream.
4 Spread chocolate butter cream over tops of 14 cakes. Remove paper cases from remaining two cakes; trim a third off the bases of the cakes, then spread tops with blue butter cream.
5 Using picture as a guide, position cakes on cake board to form the number 8; secure each with a little butter cream.

6 Using the blade of a hot metal spatula, melt long edges of the Cherry Ripe bar; attach the two Curly Wurly bars on either side of the Cherry Ripe to make a bridge. Stand a few minutes to set; position on blue cakes.
7 Cut licorice strap into thin strips; using picture as a guide, use strips to make road markings. Cut licorice into thicker strips to make a pedestrian crossing; position the jelly baby as a pedestrian, securing with a little butter cream.
8 Cut two pieces of licorice to hold the traffic lights. Use a tiny amount of butter cream to attach the M&M's to the licorice; lay flat until firm. Attach the licorice pieces to the ice-block sticks with a little more butter cream; lay flat until firm. Position traffic lights in cakes.
9 Use the jube for a roundabout. Position the vehicles.

tip The traffic lights can be made several hours ahead; leave them flat until the butter cream is firm. Store them in the fridge, then place them on the cake at party time.

octopus eight

equipment

- 23cm x 34cm (9¼-inch x 13½-inch) number 8 cake pan
- 25cm x 40cm (10-inch x 16-inch) rectangular cake board (page 68)

cake

- 3 x 340g (11-ounce) packets butter cake mix
- 2 quantities butter cream (page 65)
- purple and aqua food colouring

decorations

- ¼ cup (35g) white chocolate Melts, melted
- 8 Killer Pythons
- 85g (3-ounce) packet blackcurrant jelly crystals
- ¼ cup (20g) desiccated coconut
- purple food colouring
- 1 black licorice strap
- 3 white chocolate Melts, extra
- 2 green Smarties

1 Preheat oven to 180°C/350°F. Grease cake pan; line base with baking paper.

2 Make cakes according to directions on packets; pour mixture into pan. Bake about 1 hour. Stand in pan 5 minutes before turning top-side up, onto a wire rack to cool.

3 Using a serrated knife, level cake top; place cake, cut-side down, on cake board, securing with a little butter cream.

4 Using the picture as a guide, draw two 3cm x 4cm (1¼-inch x 1½-inch) eyes on a sheet of baking paper; turn paper over so outlines are underneath. Place melted chocolate in piping bag. Pipe eyes onto baking paper; refrigerate until set.

5 Reserve about 1 teaspoon of butter cream. Tint half the remaining butter cream purple; spread all over cake for the head. Tint remaining butter cream aqua; spread all over remaining cake.

6 Position Pythons around octopus chin, pressing gently into butter cream.

7 Combine jelly crystals, coconut and a few drops of purple colouring in a small plastic bag; rub until evenly coloured. Sprinkle mixture over face and top of tentacles.

8 Cut licorice into thin strips; outline around the hole in the centre of the head for a mouth. Position extra Melts for teeth. Position eyes on head; position Smarties for pupils, securing with a little of the reserved butter cream.

nine lazing ladybirds

equipment

- 22cm x 34cm (9-inch x 13½-inch) number 9 cake pan
- 25cm x 40cm (10-inch x 16-inch) rectangular cake board (page 68)
- piping bag fitted with 4mm (⅛-inch) plain tube

cake

- 3 x 340g (11-ounce) packets butter cake mix
- 2 quantities butter cream (page 65)
- green food colouring

decorations

- 9 chocolate ladybirds
- 9 spearmint leaves

1 Preheat oven to 180°C/350°F. Grease cake pan; line base with baking paper.

2 Make cakes according to directions on packets; pour mixture into pan. Bake about 50 minutes. Stand in pan 5 minutes before turning top-side up, onto a wire rack to cool.

3 Using a serrated knife, level cake top; place cake, cut-side down, on cake board, securing with a little butter cream.

4 Tint butter cream green; spread three-quarters of the butter cream all over cake.

5 Tint remaining butter cream a deeper green; spoon into piping bag. Pipe vine and tendrils onto cake. Position chocolate ladybirds and spearmint leaves on cake.

jewels at nine

equipment

- 22cm x 34cm (9-inch x 13½-inch) number 9 cake pan
- 25cm x 40cm (10-inch x 16-inch) rectangular cake board (page 68)

cake

- 3 x 340g (11-ounce) packets butter cake mix
- 1 quantity fluffy frosting (page 65)
- orange food colouring

decorations

- 2 x 130g (4-ounce) packets candy jewellery

1 Preheat oven to 180°C/350°F. Grease cake pan; line base with baking paper.

2 Make cakes according to directions on packets; pour mixture into pan. Bake about 50 minutes. Stand in pan 5 minutes before turning top-side up, onto a wire rack to cool.

3 Using a serrated knife, level cake top; place cake, cut-side down, on cake board, securing with a little frosting.

4 Tint frosting pale orange; spread all over cake. Using picture as a guide, position candy jewellery on cake.

tips To keep the glossy finish to the frosting, the cake needs to be frosted no longer than 1 hour before the party. The frosting soon dries out, resembling cooked meringue. You could also decorate this cake with snake and frog lollies.

nine birthday candles

equipment

- **12-hole (⅓-cup/80ml) standard muffin pan**
- **11 purple standard muffin paper cases**
- **7cm (2¾-inch) round fluted cutter**
- **3.5cm (1½-inch) round cutter**
- **40cm x 50cm (16-inch x 20-inch) rectangular cake board (page 68)**

cake

- **1 x 340g (11-ounce) packet butter cake mix**
- **⅓ cup (110g) apricot jam, warmed, strained**
- **½ cup (80g) icing (confectioners') sugar**
- **250g (8 ounces) ready-made white icing**
- **pink and mauve food colouring**

decorations

- **5 packets purple scrapbooking flowers**
- **2 packets pink scrapbooking flowers**
- **11 tea-light candles**

1 Preheat oven to 180°C/350°F. Line muffin pan with the paper cases.

2 Make cake according to directions on packet; drop 2½ level tablespoons of the mixture into each paper case. Bake about 20 minutes. Stand cakes in pan 5 minutes before turning top-side up, onto a wire rack to cool.

3 Lightly brush jam on cake tops. Knead ready-made icing on a surface dusted with sifted icing sugar until smooth; divide into three equal portions. Tint one portion pink and one portion mauve; leave the remaining portion white. Roll out each colour, one at a time, until 3mm (⅛-inch) thick.

4 Using the 7cm (2¾-inch) cutter, cut three rounds from the pink icing, four rounds from the mauve icing and four rounds from the white icing; position on cakes. Using the 3.5cm (1½-inch) cutter, cut out the centre of each icing round; discard centre cut-outs.

5 Attach scrapbooking flowers around the side of each candle; position candle in the centre of each cake.

6 Using picture as a guide, position cakes on cake board to form the number 9; secure with a little butter cream.

tips You'll have 1 cup of the cake mixture left over; use to make extra cakes for the party. Use any themed scrapbooking stickers you like.

ten soda and pizza

equipment

- **deep 22cm (9-inch) round cake pan**
- **15cm x 25cm (6-inch x 10-inch) loaf pan**
- **35cm x 50cm (14-inch x 20-inch) rectangular cake board (page 68)**

cake

- **2 x 340g (11-ounce) packets butter cake mix**

decorations

- **500g (1 pound) ready-made white icing**
- **icing (confectioners') sugar**
- **red food colouring**
- **½ cup (160g) strawberry jam**
- **4 pieces turkish delight**
- **1 curly straw**
- **3 cake stars**
- **white glossy decorating gel**
- **1 teaspoon cocoa powder**
- **1 tablespoon water**
- **yellow food colouring**
- **¼ cup (15g) shredded coconut**
- **7 black jelly beans**
- **5 fruit fantasy strawberries**
- **1 sour apple karate belt**

1 Preheat oven to 180°C/350°F. Grease pans; line base with baking paper.

2 Make cakes according to directions on packets; pour evenly between pans to the same depth. Bake about 35 minutes. Stand in pans 5 minutes; turn onto wire racks to cool.

3 Using a serrated knife, level cake tops; turn cakes cut-side down. Using picture as a guide, cut out soda glass from loaf cake by cutting at a slight angle from top corners of the cake. Place cakes, cut-side down, on cake board.

4 On surface dusted with icing sugar, knead 290g (9-ounces) of the ready-made icing until smooth; tint red. Roll out until large enough to cover loaf cake. Cut one side of the icing straight. Carefully lift icing onto cake, placing the cut side 3cm (1¼-inch) below the top edge of the cake. Gently mould icing over cake; trim edges. Brush ¼ cup of the jam on the uniced part of the cake.

5 Roll 10g (½-ounce) of ready-made icing into a 20cm (8-inch) long cord. Position at top of soda glass to create a rim on the glass, trim ends.

6 Rinse icing sugar off turkish delight; pat dry with absorbent paper.

Cut each piece into small cubes; press onto jam at top of soda glass. Push in curly straw.

7 Decorate glass with cake stars. Using white decorating gel, pipe a swirl onto soda glass.

8 Roll 200g (6½-ounces) of ready-made icing into a 5cm x 80cm (2-inch x 32-inch) rectangle; lift and place around edge of round cake. Using hands dusted with icing sugar, gently mould icing over edge of cake, trim edge. Using a small knife, cut unevenly into icing on top of round cake. Blend cocoa powder with water in a small bowl; brush over icing for pizza crust.

9 Spread remaining jam in centre of round cake.

10 Place a few drops of yellow colouring in a small bowl with 2 teaspoons of water. Add coconut; toss gently to colour unevenly. Scatter coconut over jam on round cake for cheese; position jelly beans and strawberries. Cut karate belt into curvy strips; place randomly on pizza cake.

double digits

equipment
- **8cm x 25cm x 7cm (3¼-inch x 10-inch x 2¾-inch) bar cake pan**
- **deep 25cm (10-inch) round cake pan**
- **45cm (18-inch) square cake board (page 68)**

cake
- **4 x 340g (11-ounce) packets butter cake mix**
- **2 quantities butter cream (page 65)**
- **yellow food colouring**

decorations
- **3 x 160g (5-ounce) packets rainbow sour straps**
- **2 x 350g (11-ounce) packets jubes**

1 Preheat oven to 170°C/340°F. Grease pans; line base and side(s) with baking paper, extending the paper 5cm (2 inches) above sides.

2 Make one cake according to directions on packet; pour mixture into bar pan. Bake bar cake about 40 minutes. Stand in pan 10 minutes before turning, top-side up, onto a wire rack to cool.

3 Make remaining cakes according to directions on packets; pour mixture into round pan. Bake about 1½ hours. Stand in pan 10 minutes before turning, top-side up, onto a wire rack to cool.

4 Using a serrated knife, level cake tops so they are the same height. Cut round cake to form a 'Y' in the centre, as pictured. Trim bar cake to form the number 1, as pictured. Secure cakes to cake board with a little butter cream.

5 Tint butter cream pale yellow; spread all over both cakes.

6 To decorate sides of cakes, measure the height of the cakes; using a pair of scissors, cut the sour straps into lengths of the same height. Position the sour straps on all sides of both cakes, as pictured.

7 Using scissors, cut the jubes in half; position, cut-side up, on tops of cakes, overlapping slightly, to cover completely.

tip Be careful when cutting the jubes as they tend to stick to the knife. To avoid this, dip the knife in hot water and dry it before cutting.

tip You can make and ice the cake up to a day ahead. Store in an airtight container until required. Decorate cake with cream and grated chocolate just before serving.

laming-ten

equipment

- two 8cm x 25cm (3-inch x 10-inch) bar pan
- 20cm (8-inch) ring cake pan
- 35cm x 50cm (14-inch x 20-inch) rectangular cake board (page 68)

cake

- 2 x 340g (11-ounce) packets butter cake mix
- 3 cups (480g) icing (confectioners') sugar
- ½ cup (50g) cocoa powder
- 3 tablespoons apricot jam
- 1 cup (250ml) warm water

decorations

- 2 cups (160g) desiccated coconut
- 300ml (½ pint) pouring cream
- 30g (1 ounce) dark (semi-sweet) chocolate, grated coarsely

1 Preheat oven to 180°C/350°F. Grease pans; line base and side(s) with baking paper, extending the paper 5cm (2 inches) above sides.

2 Make cakes according to directions on packets; pour mixture evenly among pans. Bake bar pans about 25 minutes. Bake ring pan about 40 minutes. Stand in pans 10 minutes before turning, top-side up, onto wire racks to cool.

3 Using a serrated knife, level cake tops so they are the same height. Leave one bar cake whole; cut the other into three pieces (see page 72). Cut ring cake in half.

4 Sift icing sugar and cocoa into a large bowl. Gradually add combined jam and water, stirring until mixture is smooth; push through a wire sieve.

5 Pour chocolate icing into a large baking dish; sprinkle coconut on a large sheet of baking paper. Working with one piece of cake at a time, dip cake pieces into icing until evenly coated; lift out of the icing, holding above the dish 1 minute to allow excess icing to drain. Transfer cake to coconut; toss gently until completely coated. Place iced cake pieces on baking paper 10 minutes until icing is dry.

6 Assemble iced cake pieces on cake board to form number 10.

7 Beat cream in a medium bowl with an electric mixer until soft peaks form. Using picture as a guide, decoratively pipe cream on cakes; top with grated chocolate.

If you want to make your own cakes, these recipes will bake at similar times, temperatures and in the same pan sizes as the packet cakes suggested in each recipe. One quantity of each of these cake recipes is equivalent to one packet butter cake mix. All un-iced cakes can be frozen for up to 3 months.

BASIC BUTTER CAKE

- 125g (4-ounces) butter, softened
- 1 teaspoon vanilla extract
- ¾ cup (165g) caster (superfine) sugar
- 2 eggs
- 1½ cups (225g) self-raising flour
- ½ cup (125ml) milk

1 Preheat oven. Grease and line pan(s).
2 Beat butter, extract and sugar in a small bowl with electric mixer until light and fluffy. Beat in eggs, one at a time. Stir in flour and milk, in two batches. Spread into pan(s). Bake as directed.

GLUTEN-FREE BUTTER CAKE

- 100g (3 ounces) butter, softened
- 1 cup (150g) gluten-free self-raising flour
- ½ cup (110g) caster (superfine) sugar
- ¼ cup (60ml) milk
- 1 egg
- 1 egg white

1 Preheat oven. Grease and line pan(s).
2 Beat butter in a small bowl with an electric mixer until a paler colour. Beat sifted flour, 2 tablespoons of the sugar and milk into the butter, in two batches.
3 Beat egg and egg white in a small bowl with electric mixer until thick and creamy. Gradually beat in remaining sugar until dissolved. Slowly pour egg mixture into flour mixture with motor operating on low speed; beat only until combined. Spread into pan(s). Bake as directed.

QUICK CHOCOLATE CAKE

- 1⅓ cups (200g) self-raising flour
- ½ cup (50g) cocoa powder
- 125g (4 ounces) butter, softened
- ½ teaspoon vanilla extract
- 1¼ cups (275g) caster (superfine) sugar
- 2 eggs
- ⅔ cup (160ml) water

1 Preheat oven. Grease and line pan(s).
2 Sift flour and cocoa into a medium bowl, add remaining ingredients; beat on low speed with an electric mixer until ingredients are just combined. Increase speed to medium; beat 3 minutes or until mixture is smooth and changed to a lighter colour. Spread into pan(s). Bake as directed.

cakes & icings

BUTTER CREAM

- **125g (4 ounces) butter, softened**
- **1½ cups (240g) icing (confectioners') sugar**
- **2 tablespoons milk**

1 Beat butter in a small bowl with an electric mixer until as white as possible.

2 Gradually beat in half the sifted icing sugar, milk, then remaining icing sugar.

chocolate variation Sift ⅓ cup (35g) cocoa powder in with the first batch of icing sugar.

coloured variations Start to tint butter cream (or any icing) by dipping a skewer into the bottle of colouring, shaking off the excess, then dipping the skewer into the icing; beat well with a wooden spoon. Every bottle of colouring will vary in strength; by adding it gradually with a skewer you avoid over-colouring. Make sure the colouring is beaten evenly through the butter cream. See also page 69.

FLUFFY FROSTING

- **1 cup (220g) caster (superfine) sugar**
- **⅓ cup (80ml) water**
- **2 egg whites**

1 Stir sugar and the water in a small saucepan over high heat, without boiling, until sugar is dissolved. Boil, uncovered, without stirring, about 5 minutes or until syrup reaches 114°C (240°F) on a candy thermometer. Remove from heat, allow bubbles to subside.

2 Begin to beat the egg whites in a small bowl with an electric mixer on a medium speed towards the end of the syrup's cooking time. Keep beating egg whites while sugar syrup reaches the correct temperature, or the egg white will deflate.

3 With the mixer on medium speed, slowly pour in the hot syrup in a thin, steady stream; if the syrup is added too quickly, the frosting will not thicken. Once all the syrup is added, continue beating on medium speed for 10 minutes or until the mixture is thick and stands in stiff peaks; the frosting should be barely warm at this stage. Use immediately. See also page 70.

coloured variations Beat small amounts of colouring through the frosting during mixing, or by stirring it in with a spatula at the end. See also page 70.

READY-MADE ICING

Ready-made icing is available from supermarkets and cake-decorating suppliers. To use, break off as much icing as you need; re-wrap remaining icing to exclude the air or a crust will develop, which will spoil the smooth texture of the icing. Knead icing on a surface dusted with sifted icing sugar. To colour the icing, work tiny amounts of the colouring through the icing at a time. The icing should be smooth and free from stickiness. Only work with small amounts of icing at a time as the air will dry it out. Cover any rolled-out icing with plastic wrap. See also page 70.

CAKE PANS

There's a vast array of cake pans available from chain stores, supermarkets, cookware shops and cake decorating suppliers. Price is a guide to quality and if you buy wisely and look after the pans, they should last a lifetime. Cake pans are made from many different materials – uncoated aluminium, which is our favourite, are becoming increasingly hard to find. There are metal pans with non-stick coating, which still need greasing, scratch easily and tend to make baked goods develop a heavy crust (reduce the oven temperature to compensate). Heavy good-quality tin pans bake cakes well, but usually work better if baked at a slightly lower temperature than normal. Inexpensive cake pans made from thin flimsy tin tend to twist and buckle, often after the first time they're used. Cakes baked in silicone pans develop a light crust, which is sometimes a good thing. Muffins and cupcakes work well in these pans.

CAKE BOARDS

Cake boards not only form part of the decoration, but make the cake easier to handle. Place the cake, as directed, on a board that has been covered with decorative greaseproof paper, contact, or any type of patterned foil-like gift wrapping. We've given an approximate cake-board size in all of the recipes, allowing some space around the cake. Using masonite or a similarly strong board, cut your selected paper 5-10cm (2-4 inches) larger than the shape of the board. Boards, in a variety of sizes, can be bought, already covered, from cake-decorating suppliers and some craft shops. See page 68 for tips on covering a board.

PACKET OR HOMEMADE CAKES

Unbaked cake mixtures (packet and homemade) will tolerate standing at a cool room temperature for at least an hour before baking. We have used cakes made from packet mixes in this book for consistency of size and baking times. While we used 340g (11-ounce) packets, there are other sizes available and they will all work with our recipes. If you want to make your own cakes, choose any of the recipes on page 64; they will bake at similar temperatures, times, and in the same pan sizes as the packet mix cakes suggested in each recipe. All un-iced cakes can be frozen for up to 3 months.

BEATING PACKET MIXES

It's important to beat the packet mixes properly using an electric mixer – not a food processor or blender. We found a stand-alone mixer gave us the best results, simply because it's easier to let the machine do the work rather than holding a hand-held mixer (there is a tendency to under-beat the mixture using one of these). Also, it's important to beat the packet mixes enough to develop the volume of the

baking information

mixture. For best results, have the ingredients to be added at room temperature, start the mixer at a low speed to incorporate the ingredients, then gradually increase speed to medium. As a rule, one packet of cake mix fits into a small bowl, two or three packets into a medium bowl, and four packets into a large bowl. The beaters should always be well down into the mixture to create volume.

BAKING

We used conventional oven temperatures in this book; if you use a fan-forced oven, decrease the temperature by 10-20 degrees. Fan-forced ovens should bake everything that is being cooked in the oven evenly, however, some domestic ovens have hot spots. If you have to bake cakes on two oven racks, you need to change the positions of the cakes about halfway through baking time. It's fine to cook more than one cake on the same rack, but the cake

pans shouldn't touch each other, the sides of the oven or the closed oven door. It's usually a good idea to change the positions of the cake pans on the same rack, too. Allow for the cake to rise when positioning racks before the oven is preheated. As a guide, cakes should be baked in the centre of the oven, towards the lower half of the oven. If the oven is loaded with cakes of varying sizes, they might take a little longer to bake than our recipes indicate.

MEASURING CAKE QUANTITIES

To achieve the same results as we did for the cakes in this book, it's important to measure the mixture accurately into the correct-sized cake pans. Often there is some cake mixture left over, just use it to make more cakes for the party. Some of the cakes in this book require half-packets of cake mixture to be used; make the whole cake mix then use half the mixture, as

indicated by the recipe, and use the remaining mixture to make additional patty or cupcakes for the party.

FOOD COLOURINGS

Use good-quality colourings for the best results; they will 'hold' the colour in the icing. Some of the inexpensive liquid colourings will fade or darken the icing on standing. Icings or frostings based on butter are the most difficult to colour as butter is yellow, so any colour will be affected by the base colour. This is why it's important to beat the butter until it's as white as possible. We found unsalted butter to work (and taste) the best. Fluffy frosting is one of the easiest to colour, because it's white to begin with. Coloured icings can change on standing, particularly if you're using liquid colourings. If possible (it's not with fluffy frosting), colour a small portion of the icing to the shade you want, keep it airtight, and let it stand for a few hours before colouring the whole batch.

COVERING A SQUARE BOARD Place board, top-side down, on the back of covering paper with a 5cm border. Glue or tape paper; cover as you would a book.

COVERING A ROUND BOARD Snip paper border, on an angle, all around. Fold each snipped piece of paper onto the board; tape or glue each piece on the board.

GREASING CAKE PANS Melted butter, applied evenly with a pastry brush, is the best method of greasing a pan, particularly if it's of an unusual shape or patterned.

LINING A ROUND PAN (1) Cut a 7cm-wide length of baking paper long enough to encircle inside the pan with an overlap. Fold 2cm over one side, snip on an angle.

LINING A ROUND PAN (2) Position the snipped lining paper inside greased pan. Cut a round of baking paper using the base of the pan as a guide; position in pan.

LINING A SQUARE PAN Cut strips of baking paper long enough to cover base and sides. Always extend the paper over each side by about 5cm.

LEVELLING CAKES

Most cakes need to have their tops cut off so they sit flat on a cake board or plate. Use a large sharp serrated knife to do this.

PREPARING TO DECORATE

Most cakes are turned top-side down for decorating. Recipes will indicate when to position the cake on a cake board or plate.

BRUSHING WITH JAM

Use warmed, sieved jam to brush over the surface of the cake. If the cake is fresh and crumbly, freeze it for an hour or so to make the job easier.

TINTING BUTTER CREAM

Use a skewer to dab a tiny amount of food colouring onto the butter cream; mix it through thoroughly before adding any more.

APPLYING BUTTER CREAM

(1) If the cake is fresh, freeze it for a few hours first. Using a spatula, apply a very thin layer of butter cream to form an "undercoat".

APPLYING BUTTER CREAM

(2) Spread the final layer of butter cream evenly over the "undercoat".

MAKING FLUFFY FROSTING Gradually pour the hot syrup into stiffly beaten egg whites in a thin steady stream. Beat until firm peaks form.

TINTING FLUFFY FROSTING Beat colouring into frosting just before you're about to use it. This frosting sets on standing so use it quickly.

TINTING READY-MADE WHITE ICING Start with a tiny dab of colouring, working it through the icing until evenly coloured. Add more colouring as desired.

CUTTING SHAPES FROM READY-MADE ICING Roll the icing to the correct thickness. Use sharp cutters to cut out shapes. Dry shapes on baking paper.

TINTING COCONUT Wearing gloves, rub drops of colouring through coconut in a small bowl until evenly coloured. You can also use this method with sugar.

TINTING SUGAR Massage colouring through sugar in a strong, resealable plastic bag until it's evenly coloured. You can also use this method with coconut.

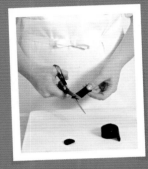

USING LICORICE
Use a pair of sharp scissors for cutting and trimming licorice into various shapes and sizes.

MELTING CHOCOLATE
Melt chocolate over hot water; make sure the water in the pan doesn't touch the bottom of the bowl, so the chocolate doesn't overheat.

PIPING CHOCOLATE
Use small piping bags fitted with a plain tube, or a paper piping bag. Half-fill the bag with melted chocolate; pipe shapes onto a lined tray.

PAPER PIPING BAGS
Cut a square from a sheet of baking paper, fold it in half diagonally, cut it in half along the fold to make two triangles.

SHAPING PIPING BAGS
Hold the apex of the triangle towards you, wrap one point around to form a cone shape; wriggle the three triangle points until they line up.

SECURING PIPING BAGS
Staple the piping bag to hole the three points of the triangle in place. Half-fill the bag, then snip a tiny piece from the point of the bag.

step-by-step

NUMBER ONE (1)
Leave one bar cake whole. Cut the other bar cake into three pieces, as pictured.

NUMBER ONE (2)
Assemble the cake pieces, cut-side down, on a cake board to form the number 1. Discard remaining piece.

NUMBER TWO (PAGE 15)
Cut number 2 shaped cake into lots of jigsaw pieces, as pictured.

NUMBER SIX (PAGE 39)
Shape the tail portion of the number 6 cake into a curvy devil's tail, making a point at the end.

NUMBER TEN (PAGE 63)
(1) Leave one bar cake whole. Cut the other bar cake into three pieces, as pictured. Cut the ring cake in half.

NUMBER TEN (2)
Assemble the cake pieces, cut-side down, on a cake board to form the number 10. Discard remaining piece.

use as a 6 or 9

this piece
converts the
8 to a 3

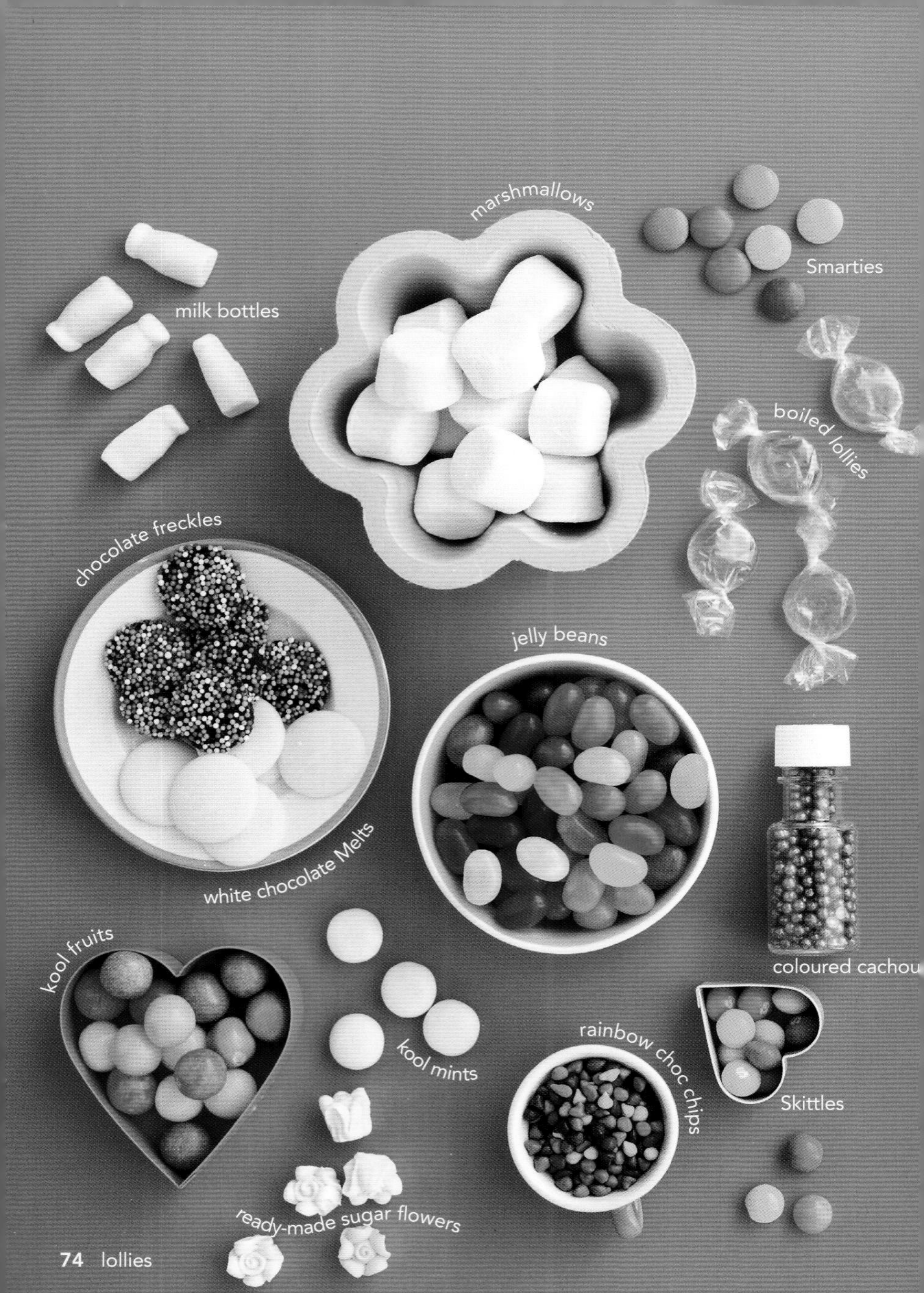

marshmallows

Smarties

milk bottles

boiled lollies

chocolate freckles

jelly beans

white chocolate Melts

coloured cachou

kool fruits

rainbow choc chips

kool mints

Skittles

ready-made sugar flowers

lollies

-cream wafers

jubes

red sour strap

mini M&M's

mini mallows

jelly babies

fruit sticks

hundreds and thousands

teevee snacks

ready-made sugar flowers

bananas

black licorice strap

silver cachous

candy jewellery

ALMONDS
blanched brown skins removed.

flaked paper-thin slices.

ground also called almond meal; nuts are powdered to a coarse flour texture for use in baking or as a thickening agent.

BAKING PAPER also called parchment paper or baking parchment, a silicone-coated paper primarily used for lining baking pans and trays so cakes won't stick, making removal easy.

BAKING POWDER a raising agent consisting mainly of two parts cream of tartar to one part bicarbonate of soda.

gluten-free suitable for people with an allergic response to glutens or as an alternative to everyday baking powder.

BICARBONATE OF SODA also called baking soda.

BUTTER use salted or unsalted (sweet) butter; 125g is equal to one stick (4 ounces).

CACHOUS also called dragées in some countries; minuscule metallic-looking-but-edible confectionery balls used in cake decorating; available in silver, gold or various colours.

CAKE BOARDS often made from masonite and covered in a thick non-absorbable paper; silver or gold coloured. Come in myriad sizes, usually round or square. If displaying on a cake board, the base board is often 10-15cm larger than the cake, so it can be lifted and transported without fingers poking holes in the icing.

CHOCOLATE
Choc Bits also known as chocolate chips or chocolate morsels; available in milk, white and dark chocolate. Made of cocoa liquor, cocoa butter, sugar and an emulsifier; they hold their shape when baked – ideal for decorating.

choc Melts discs of compounded milk, white or dark chocolate ideal for melting and moulding.

dark (semi-sweet) also known as luxury chocolate; made of a high percentage of cocoa liquor and cocoa butter, and little added sugar.

milk most popular eating chocolate, mild and very sweet; similar in make-up to dark chocolate, with the difference being the addition of milk solids.

white contains no cocoa solids but derives its sweet flavour from cocoa butter. Very sensitive to heat

CINNAMON available as sticks (quills) and ground into powder; one of the world's most common spices.

COCOA POWDER also known as unsweetened cocoa; cocoa beans (cacao seeds) that have been fermented, roasted, shelled, then ground into a powder.

COCONUT
desiccated concentrated, dried, unsweetened and finely shredded coconut flesh.

essence synthetically produced from flavouring, oil and alcohol.

flaked dried flaked coconut flesh.

shredded unsweetened thin strips of dried coconut flesh.

CONFECTIONERY
allsorts layered sweets consisting of licorice and fondant.

bullets small lengths of licorice coated in chocolate candy.

licorice an aniseed-flavoured confection which comes in straps, tubes and twisted ropes.

Mallow Bakes coloured marshmallow pellets; made from sugar, glucose, cornflour and gelatine.

marshmallows pink and white; made from sugar, glucose, cornflour and gelatine.

Smarties made from chocolate, sugar and flour.

spearmint leaves soft sugar-coated leaf-shaped sweets flavoured with spearmint.

CORN SYRUP a sweet syrup made by heating cornstarch with water under pressure. It comes in light and dark types and is used in baking and in confectionery making.

CORNFLOUR (CORNSTARCH) used as a thickening agent. Wheaten cornflour is made from wheat rather than corn (maize) and gives sponge cakes a lighter texture (due to the fact wheaten cornflour has some gluten).

CREAM
pouring also known as pure cream. It has no additives and contains a minimum fat content of 35%.

thickened (heavy) a whipping cream containing a thickener. Minimum fat content 35%.

CREAM OF TARTAR the acid ingredient in baking powder; added to confectionery mixtures to help prevent sugar from crystallising. Keeps frostings creamy and improves volume when beating egg whites.

CUTTERS come in many sizes, shapes, styles, plunging etc. Used to cut ready-made icing into different shapes.

EGGS we use large chicken eggs weighing an average of 60g. If a recipe calls for raw or barely cooked eggs, exercise caution if there is a salmonella problem in your area.

FLORISTS' WIRE also called floral or craft wire. A covered flexible wire that comes in different thicknesses. Used to position shapes or flowers on a cake.

FLOUR

plain (all-purpose) unbleached wheat flour; is the best for baking as the gluten content ensures a strong dough for a light result.

self-raising plain flour sifted with baking powder in the proportion of 1 cup flour to 2 teaspoons baking powder.

FOOD COLOURING a vegetable-based substance available in liquid, paste or gel form. Used to colour icings, cake mixtures or sugar.

GELATINE a thickening agent. Available in sheet form (leaf geletine) or as a powder –

3 teaspoons powdered gelatine (8g or one sachet) is roughly equivalent to four gelatine leaves.

GREASING PANS use butter, margarine, oil or cooking-oil spray to grease baking pans; over-greasing pans can cause food to overbrown. Use absorbent paper or a pastry brush to spread the oil or butter over the pan. Try covering your hand with a small plastic bag then swiping it into the butter or margarine.

HUNDREDS & THOUSANDS also known as 100's & 1000's; tiny sugar-syrup-coated sugar crystals in a variety of colours.

JAM also called conserve or preserve.

JELLY CRYSTALS a combination of sugar, gelatine, colours and flavours; when dissolved in water, the solution sets as firm jelly.

LOLLIES also called sweets or candy.

MILK we use full-cream homogenised milk unless otherwise specified.

OIL, COOKING SPRAY we use a cholesterol-free made from canola oil.

READY-MADE WHITE ICING also called soft icing, ready-to-roll and prepared fondant. Available from major supermarkets in the baking section.

ROASTING/TOASTING nuts and dried coconut can be roasted in the oven to restore their fresh flavour and release their aromatic essential oils.

Spread evenly onto an oven tray then roast in a moderate oven for about 5 minutes. Desiccated coconut, pine nuts and sesame seeds roast more evenly if stirred over low heat in a heavy-based frying pan; their natural oils will help turn them golden brown.

SUGAR

brown a soft, finely granulated sugar retaining molasses for its characteristic colour and flavour.

caster (superfine) finely granulated table sugar.

icing (confectioners') also called powdered sugar; pulverised granulated sugar crushed together with a small amount of cornflour.

pure icing (confectioners') also called powdered sugar.

raw natural brown granulated sugar.

TEMPERING the process by which chocolate is melted at a specific temperature that enables it to set with a glossy finish.

VANILLA

bean dried, long, thin pod from a tropical golden orchid; the minuscule black seeds inside the bean are used to impart a luscious vanilla flavour in baking and desserts. Place a whole bean in a jar of sugar to make vanilla sugar.

extract made by extracting the flavour from the vanilla bean pod; pods are soaked, usually in alcohol, to capture the authentic flavour.

conversion chart

measures

One Australian metric measuring cup holds approximately 250ml, one Australian metric tablespoon holds 20ml, one Australian metric teaspoon holds 5ml. The difference between one country's measuring cups and another's is within a 2- or 3-teaspoon variance, and will not affect your cooking results. North America, New Zealand and the United Kingdom use a 15ml tablespoon. All cup and spoon measurements are level. The most accurate way of measuring dry ingredients is to weigh them. When measuring liquids, use a clear glass or plastic jug with metric markings. We use large eggs with an average weight of 60g.

dry measures

METRIC	IMPERIAL
15g	½oz
30g	1oz
60g	2oz
90g	3oz
125g	4oz (¼lb)
155g	5oz
185g	6oz
220g	7oz
250g	8oz (½lb)
280g	9oz
315g	10oz
345g	11oz
375g	12oz (¾lb)
410g	13oz
440g	14oz
470g	15oz
500g	16oz (1lb)
750g	24oz (1½lb)
1kg	32oz (2lb)

liquid measures

METRIC	IMPERIAL
30ml	1 fluid oz
60ml	2 fluid oz
100ml	3 fluid oz
125ml	4 fluid oz
150ml	5 fluid oz
190ml	6 fluid oz
250ml	8 fluid oz
300ml	10 fluid oz
500ml	16 fluid oz
600ml	20 fluid oz
1000ml (1 litre)	1¾ pints

length measures

METRIC	IMPERIAL
3mm	⅛in
6mm	¼in
1cm	½in
2cm	¾in
2.5cm	1in
5cm	2in
6cm	2½in
8cm	3in
10cm	4in
13cm	5in
15cm	6in
18cm	7in
20cm	8in
23cm	9in
25cm	10in
28cm	11in
30cm	12in (1ft)

oven temperatures

These oven temperatures are only a guide for conventional ovens. For fan-forced ovens, check the manufacturer's manual.

	°C (CELSIUS)	°F (FAHRENHEIT)
Very slow	120	250
Slow	150	300
Moderately slow	160	325
Moderate	180	350
Moderately hot	200	400
Hot	220	425
Very hot	240	475

The imperial measurements used in these recipes are approximate only. Measurements for cake pans are approximate only. Using same-shaped cake pans of a similar size should not affect the outcome of your baking. We measure the inside top of the cake pan to determine sizes.

Published in 2013 by Bauer Media Books, Sydney
Bauer Media Books are published by Bauer Media Limited
54 Park St, Sydney
GPO Box 4088, Sydney, NSW 2001.
phone (02) 9282 8618; fax (02) 9126 3702
www.awwcookbooks.com.au

MEDIA GROUP

BAUER MEDIA BOOKS
Publishing Director - Gerry Reynolds
Publisher - Sally Wright
Editorial & Food Director - Pamela Clark
Director of Sales, Marketing & Rights - Brian Cearnes
Creative Director - Hieu Chi Nguyen
Food Concept Director - Sophia Young

Published and Distributed in the United Kingdom by Octopus Publishing Group
Endeavour House
189 Shaftesbury Avenue
London WC2H 8JY
United Kingdom
phone (+44)(0)207 632 5400; fax (+44)(0)207 632 5405
info@octopus-publishing.co.uk;
www.octopusbooks.co.uk

Printed by 1010 Printing International Limited, China.

International foreign language rights, Brian Cearnes, Bauer Media Books
bcearnes@bauer-media.com.au

A catalogue record for this book is available from the British Library.
ISBN 978-1-74245-380-4
© Bauer Media Limited 2013
ABN 18 053 273 546